SPACE FLIGHT ADVENTURES AND DISASTERS

THE GEMINI 4 SPACEWALK MISSION

A MyReportLinks.com Book

CARL R. GREEN

MyReportLinks.com Books
an imprint of
 Enslow Publishers, Inc.
Box 398, 40 Industrial Road
Berkeley Heights, NJ 07922
USA

MyReportLinks.com Books, an imprint of Enslow Publishers, Inc. MyReportLinks®
is a registered trademark of Enslow Publishers, Inc.

Library of Congress Cataloging-in-Publication Data

Green, Carl R.
  The Gemini 4 spacewalk mission / Carl R. Green.
     p. cm. — (Space flight adventures and disasters)
Summary: Describes the Gemini 4 mission in 1965 when astronauts Edward
White and James McDivitt carried out the first extravehicular activity
in the United States manned space program.
Includes bibliographical references and index.
  ISBN 0-7660-5163-3
  1. Project Gemini (U.S.)—History—Juvenile literature. [1. Project
Gemini (U.S.) 2. Extravehicular activity (Manned space flight) 3. Manned
space flight. 4. White, Edward Higgins, 1930-1967. 5. McDivitt, James
Alton, 1929-] I. Title. II. Series.
  TL789.8.U6G357 2004
  629.45'84—dc22

                              2003016484

Printed in the United States of America.

10 9 8 7 6 5 4 3 2 1

To Our Readers:
Through the purchase of this book, you and your library gain access to the Report Links that specifically back up this book.

The Publisher will provide access to the Report Links that back up this book and will keep these Report Links up to date on **www.myreportlinks.com** for three years from the book's first publication date.

We have done our best to make sure all Internet addresses in this book were active and appropriate when we went to press. However, the author and the Publisher have no control over, and assume no liability for, the material available on those Internet sites or on other Web sites they may link to.

The usage of the MyReportLinks.com Books Web site is subject to the terms and conditions stated on the Usage Policy Statement on **www.myreportlinks.com**.

A password may be required to access the Report Links that back up this book. The password is found on the bottom of page 4 of this book.

Any comments or suggestions can be sent by e-mail to comments@myreportlinks.com or to the address on the back cover.

Contents

MyReportLinks.com Books
Great Books, Great Links, Great for Research!

The Report Links listed on the following four pages can save you hours of research time by **instantly** bringing you to the best Web sites relating to your report topic.

How to Use MyReportLinks.com

1 Got a Report to do?

2 Check out a MyReportLinks.com Book at the Library.

3 Read the Book.

4 Go to www.myreportlinks.com for Quick, Safe, and Up-to-Date Links!

5 Internet Report Links = Great Information.

6 Write Your Report. Impress Your Teacher.

MAX LYNX

The pre-evaluated Web sites are your links to source documents, photographs, illustrations, and maps. They also provide links to dozens—even hundreds—of Web sites about your report subject.

MyReportLinks.com Books and the MyReportLinks.com Web site save you time and make report writing easier than ever!

Please see "To Our Readers" on the copyright page for important information about this book, the MyReportLinks.com Web site, and the Report Links that back up this book. Please enter **FGE7733** if asked for a password.

Report Links

> The Internet sites described below can be accessed at
> http://www.myreportlinks.com

*EDITOR'S CHOICE

▶**National Aeronautics and Space Administration**
At the National Aeronautics and Space Administration Web site you
can learn all about NASA, including past and future space missions,
news and events, and much more.

*EDITOR'S CHOICE

▶**JSC Digital Image Collection: *Gemini* Project**
This Web site allows you to browse through images of the astronauts
who flew *Gemini* missions *3* through *12*. Each striking image is
accompanied by a brief description.

*EDITOR'S CHOICE

▶**Biographical Data: James A. McDivitt**
At this Web site you will find a brief biography of James A. McDivitt.
You will learn about his life, education, special honors, and
his contributions to NASA and the space program.

*EDITOR'S CHOICE

▶**Biographical Data: Edward H. White II**
Visit this Web site to find a brief biography of Edward H. White.
The site describes White's life, education, special honors,
NASA experience, and tragic death in 1967.

*EDITOR'S CHOICE

▶***Gemini-4* (4)**
At this Web site you can read a basic overview of *Gemini 4,* and the first
spacewalk mission. The site lists the crew members and describes the
mission objectives.

*EDITOR'S CHOICE

▶**Milestones of Flight**
The National Air and Space Museum Web site provides a time
line of historic moments in the history of flight. Visit the site to
find information that puts *Gemini 4* in perspective with other
landmark flights.

Report Links

The Internet sites described below can be accessed at http://www.myreportlinks.com

▶**Alexei Arkhipovich Leonov**

At the NASA Biographies Web site you will find a brief profile of Alexei Arkhipovich Leonov, the Russian cosmonaut who made the world's first spacewalk in 1962.

▶**The *Apollo* Program**

The *Apollo* Program Web site offers information about all of the *Apollo* missions, including the moon landings. You will also learn about the spacecraft, the astronauts, and other insider details.

▶**Biographical Data: Frank Borman**

At this Web site you can read a brief biography about Frank Borman, who was a member of the back-up crew for the *Gemini 4* mission. You will learn about his life and career at NASA.

▶**Biographical Data: James A. Lovell**

At this Web site you can read a brief biography about James A. Lovell, the second member of the back-up crew for the *Gemini 4* mission. As with the other biography sites, you will learn about his life and career at NASA.

▶**Cold War Experience: Technology**

The Cold War Experience Web site explores the ways in which the Cold War sparked innovation among scientists and inventors. You will also find an interactive time line that documents the space race.

▶**Columbus of the Cosmos**

At the Space Kids Web site you can read a brief profile of Yuri Gagarin, the first man to orbit the earth in a space capsule.

▶***Gemini*: Kennedy Space Center**

The Kennedy Space Center Web site helps you explore all of the manned and unmanned *Gemini* missions. You will also learn about the goals of the missions and the achievements of each flight.

▶***Gemini 4***

At this Web site you will find an overview of the *Gemini 4* mission, including observations made by the crew and reports on the human life experiments they conducted.

Report Links

**The Internet sites described below can be accessed at
http://www.myreportlinks.com**

▶**Gemini Program**

On this site, you can read detailed accounts of all the *Gemini* space missions.

▶**Great Images in NASA**

The Great Images in NASA Web site lets you browse through many
images of human exploration, including the famous photo of Ed White,
the first American spacewalker.

▶**Humans in Space: *Gemini 4***

At the Humans in Space Web site you will find an image of *Gemini 4,*
accompanied by a brief description of the mission. You will also find interesting
links to other space-related Web sites.

▶**Human Space Flight**

NASA's Human Space Flight Web site helps you learn about space shuttles,
and space stations, as well as providing a look at behind-the-scenes events
and space news.

▶**JSC at 40**

At the Johnson Space Center Web site you can explore forty years of
space flight history. Browse through images and read about historic moments
in the race to put astronauts on the moon.

▶***Mercury***

The *Mercury* Web site introduces you to Project *Mercury*—its goals,
the spacecraft, and the successes of this pioneer space project.

▶**NASA History Office**

At the NASA History Office you can read about NASA's history from its
beginnings in 1958 to the present. You will also learn of NASA's many
accomplishments and explore a wide variety of space topics, including the
Gemini 4 mission.

▶**NASA Kids**

The NASA Kids Web site lets you explore "Rockets and Airplanes,"
"Earth," "Astronauts Living in Space," "Space and Beyond," and many
other interesting topics.

Report Links

The Internet sites described below can be accessed at http://www.myreportlinks.com

▶**NASA Manned Rocket Missions**

At this ThinkQuest Web site you can read overviews of many NASA manned space missions, including *Gemini 4*.

▶**NASA Mission Summaries**

The NASA Mission Summaries Web site provides overviews of all its missions, including the *Gemini* series.

▶**NASA Quest**

NASA Quest is an educational Web site designed to assist kids in learning about space exploration.

▶**Project *Gemini***

At this Web site you will find overviews of the manned and unmanned *Gemini* missions. You will also find flight summaries that help you learn about the objectives of the missions and the spacecraft.

▶**Space Race**

At the Space Race Web site you will learn about the Cold War and how it fueled a race between the United States and the Soviet Union to land a man on the moon.

▶**Space Stations**

PBS's Space Station Web site provides extensive information about space stations. You will learn about their construction and their purpose, plus other interesting facts about space and space history.

▶**The White House and Space Exploration**

At the White House Historical Association Web site you will find a brief history of space exploration and the role our presidents have played in making it possible.

▶***World Almanac for Kids Online*: Human Space Flight**

The *World Almanac for Kids Online* Web site provides a brief overview of the history of human space exploration.

Gemini 4 Facts

Gemini 4 Spacecraft	Reentry module: height 12.14 ft (3.7 m); diameter 90 in (2.3 m) Weight at splashdown: 4,850 lbs (2,200 kg)
Manufacturer	McDonnell Aircraft Corporation
Launch Vehicle	Titan II rocket: First stage generates 430,000 lbs (195,045 kg) of thrust; second stage generates 100,000 lbs (45,359 kg) of thrust.
Astronauts	James A. McDivitt, Commander Edward H. White II, Pilot
Gemini Project Goals	(1) To build toward the *Apollo* moon landing by testing equipment and mission procedures. (2) To demonstrate that astronauts could survive prolonged periods of weightlessness while carrying out docking maneuvers, scientific experiments, and EVAs.
Flight Statistics	Launch—June 3, 1965 Splashdown—June 7, 1965 (4.08 days) Total distance traveled in space: 1,609,700 miles (2,590,561 km)
Orbital Data	62 orbits. perigee 100 miles (162 km); apogee 175 miles (281 km) Traveling at a speed of 17,500 mph (28,164 kmh), the spacecraft circled the earth every 90 minutes
White's EVA	Thirty-six minutes from hatch opening to closing; his spacewalk lasted 21 minutes

The Gemini 4 *mission patch.*

AN AMERICAN SPACEWALK

The year was 1965. It was the era of the Cold War, a time of intense rivalry between the United States and the Soviet Union. Which system would triumph, democracy or communism? In the military realm, the race was on to build more destructive weapons. In science, the challenge lay in blazing new trails in space. The Russians had jumped out in front by launching the first space satellite in 1957. Eight years later, the United States still was playing catch-up.

On June 3, 1965, a Titan II rocket blasted the *Gemini 4* spacecraft into orbit. The ship carried two American astronauts: Command Pilot Jim McDivitt and Pilot Ed White. Ten weeks earlier, the Russian cosmonaut Alexei Leonov had made headlines by taking a ten-minute "walk" in space. Now, as McDivitt ran down the checklist, White was suiting up for his own spacewalk. His bosses at NASA (the National Aeronautics and Space Administration) called it an EVA (Extra Vehicular Activity). Each piece of equipment had been checked and rechecked in the lab. Now, the real test was at hand. Would White's suit and tether safeguard him while he roamed the cold vacuum of space?

▶ Popping the Hatch

After assembling a 7.5-pound (3.4 kilograms) gas gun, White hooked up his 25-foot (7.6 meters) gold-braided tether. Along with providing oxygen, the tether kept him moored to the ship. Next came the emergency oxygen pack. When he

▲ *Pilot Edward White (left) and Command Pilot James McDivitt (right) flash big grins after suiting up for their first flight on June 3, 1965.*

finished, McDivitt told Mission Control that all systems checked out. From Houston, the reply flashed back. CapCom (the Capsule Command Communicator) told White, "We're ready to have you get out whenever you're ready."[1]

The astronauts quickly reduced the cabin pressure to zero. White then stood up in his seat and tried to pop the hatch—only to find that it was stuck. When the balky cover did fly open, he had to hold on tight to keep it from banging against the hull. Now, with his head poking out of the hatch, White set up a camera to record his spacewalk. As the world waited, he double-checked his work. "I wanted to make sure I didn't leave the lens cap on," he said later.[2]

▲ This is the first photo taken of Ed White's twenty-two-minute spacewalk. The camera caught him backing away from the Gemini spacecraft as he soared over the Pacific Ocean, northeast of Hawaii.

▶ Taking Some "Big Steps"

Twelve minutes after popping the hatch, White floated free of the ship. With his eyes shielded from glare by a gold-coated faceplate, he set out to explore his silent world. A pull on the tether sent him looping toward the rear of the ship. A burst from the gas gun brought him back when he came too close to the ship's thrusters. For one confusing moment, White felt as though he was moving in all directions at once. Another burst from the gas gun put him into a controlled turn, and a second burst stopped the movement. At that point, to the spacewalker's dismay, the gun ran out of gas.[3]

Like his ship, the human satellite was speeding through space at some 17,500 miles (28,000 km) per hour. As he drifted, White described the dazzling earthscape below him. In Houston, Mission Control relayed his words around the globe. "Right now I'm standing on my head and I'm looking down . . . and I'm going into a slow rotation," he told his spellbound listeners. "There is absolutely no disorientation associated with it. I can sit out here and see the whole California coast."[4] Later, talking to reporters, White recalled, "I was taking some big steps . . . the first on Hawaii, then California, Texas, Florida, and the last on the Bahamas and Bermuda."[5]

Inside *Gemini*, McDivitt had his work cut out for him. "When Ed . . . starts whipping around, it sure makes the craft tough to control," he said. The command pilot also had to be careful not to fire the control thrusters too close to the spacewalker. For his part, White tried to stay out in front of *Gemini*. The tether, however, kept swinging him back toward the rear of the module. At one point, he left smears on McDivitt's windshield when he brushed

against it. "You smeared up my windshield, you dirty dog!" his friend said with a laugh.[6]

▶ Time's Up

A hundred miles below, Mission Control was watching the clock. By now, White had been in space twice as long as the Russian spacewalker. CapCom told him to end the EVA, but the astronauts were too busy chatting to hear the order. At last, McDivitt asked Houston if there were any messages. The answer came back at once: "*Gemini 4. Get back in!*"

McDivitt relayed the order. "Come on," he told White, "let's get back in here before it gets dark."

White knew better than to press his luck. As *Gemini 4* soared high over Georgia, he picked up the camera and unplugged several electrical hookups. Working carefully, he handed his air gun and the other equipment to McDivitt. Then the reluctant astronaut pulled himself back to the hatch.

"It's the saddest moment of my life," White said as he lowered himself into the tiny cabin.[7]

EMBARKING ON A GREAT ADVENTURE

Ed White's 1965 spacewalk was a much-needed triumph for American science. Just four years earlier, the space program had been shaken by some costly launch failures. The Soviet Union's program, by contrast, was roaring ahead. The gap widened again in the spring of 1961. On April 4, cosmonaut Yuri Gagarin became the first man to fly in

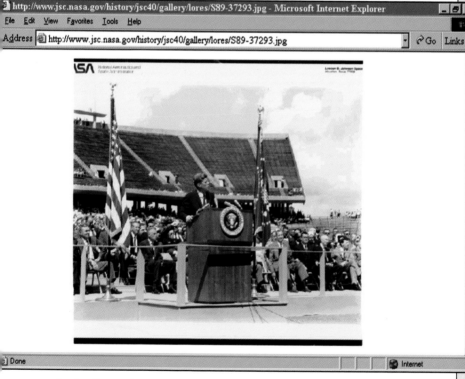

▲ On September 12, 1962, President John F. Kennedy spoke at Rice University in Texas about the American space program. In his speech, he committed the nation to the goal of landing a man on the moon.

space. His one-orbit flight, the experts agreed, gave the Soviets a big lead in the space race.

Seven weeks later, on May 25, 1961, President John F. Kennedy stepped forward to address the nation. By then astronaut Alan Shepard had ridden his *Mercury* capsule into space. Unlike the Soviet flight, NASA's planning had not allowed the capsule to orbit the Earth. Shepard's *Freedom 7* splashed down after reaching an altitude of 116 miles (187 km).[1] Even so, President Kennedy used the flight to call for an all-out effort to meet the Soviet challenge. "I believe," the young president told Congress, "that this nation should commit itself to achieving the goal, before this decade is out, of landing a man on the moon and returning him safely to earth."[2]

At the time Kennedy spoke, Americans knew that their astronauts had logged only fifteen minutes in space. They also knew that the moon project would cost billions of dollars. In the end, that did not seem to matter. The stirring words inspired the nation to embark on a grand new adventure.

▶ From *Mercury* to *Gemini*

The people who worked on the moon program understood the obstacles that lay ahead. Step by step, they had to build and test a spacecraft that could carry three astronauts into moon orbit. From there, two crew members would fly a lunar lander to the moon's surface. When their moonwalk was finished, the lander would carry the astronauts back to their mother ship.

NASA began its quest by launching a series of space missions. Each flight was designed to build on the one before. In February 1962, millions cheered as John Glenn rode his *Mercury 6* capsule to a three-orbit flight. Even though the *Mercury* program was far from finished, planners were looking ahead. Next up, they said, would be a larger spacecraft dubbed *Mercury Mark II.*

As the design took shape, NASA changed the *Mark II*'s name to "*Gemini.*" The name, Latin for "twins," was inspired by the Gemini constellation and its twin stars, Castor and Pollux. In ancient times, the two stars had been known as the patron gods of voyagers. The "twins" label also took note of *Gemini*'s two-man crews. A foot longer and a foot wider than *Mercury, Gemini*'s cabin was a full 50 percent larger.[3] No longer a "flying rock" like *Mercury,* the ship's thrusters would allow it to maneuver in space. The design pleased the newly-chosen *Gemini*

Gemini 4 - Microsoft Internet Explorer

File Edit View Favorites Tools Help

Address http://www.lsda.jsc.nasa.gov/gemini/gem4.stm   Go   Links

The objectives of the Gemini 4 (G-4) mission, though scaled down along with the originally planned duration of 7 days, included practicing rendezvous maneuvers, a tethered space walk, and several scientific experiments. Gemini 4 was launched on June 3 and landed on June 7 of 1965 with two astronauts, Ed White and James McDivitt.

G-4 was the first flight in which an Extravehicular Activity (EVA), or spacewalk, was performed by an American, astronaut Ed White. The EVA operations of Gemini 4 proved NASA's ability to engineer space suits and life support systems to sustain humans outside the protection of a spacecraft, essential for the planned future Moon landing.

The crew made many observations and completed 11 experiments during their four days in space, including studies of photography, radiation in spacecraft, simple navigation, electrostatic charge, proton/electron spectrometers and tri-Axis magnetometers . Photographic experiments recorded many geological, oceanographic, and meteorological data on

Internet

▲ *The* Gemini 4 *patch commemorates Ed White's historic EVA.*

astronauts. The new spacecraft would allow them to do what they were paid to do—fly.[4]

Long before the first ship reached the launch pad, NASA had approved a bold set of goals. If all went as planned, the *Gemini* teams would tackle six tasks:

- Test the effects of prolonged spaceflight on both crew and spacecraft.
- Check out crew rest and work cycles, eating schedules, and real-time flight planning.
- Test EVA equipment and procedures.
- Rendezvous and dock with a second space vehicle.
- Maneuver the ship in space and hit a precise landing point during reentry.
- Carry out scientific experiments.[5]

By the time *Gemini 4* soared skyward, the project was closing in on all of these goals.

▶ Training the *Gemini* Astronauts

NASA set high standards when it picked the *Gemini* astronauts. As with *Mercury*, only young, well-trained test pilots could hope to be chosen. Test pilots, NASA believed, had the skills needed to fly a spacecraft. Each candidate also had to have a college degree in engineering or one of the physical sciences. Without this training, the astronauts would find it hard to communicate with the project's engineers and scientists. Height was also a factor. Because the cockpit was a tight fit, no one taller than six feet could apply. As a final hurdle, the volunteers had to pass a series of tough physical exams.[6]

In 1962, nine *Gemini* astronauts were chosen from over two hundred candidates. A second group of fourteen joined them a year later. Once chosen, the astronauts plunged into their training program. Long, tough sessions

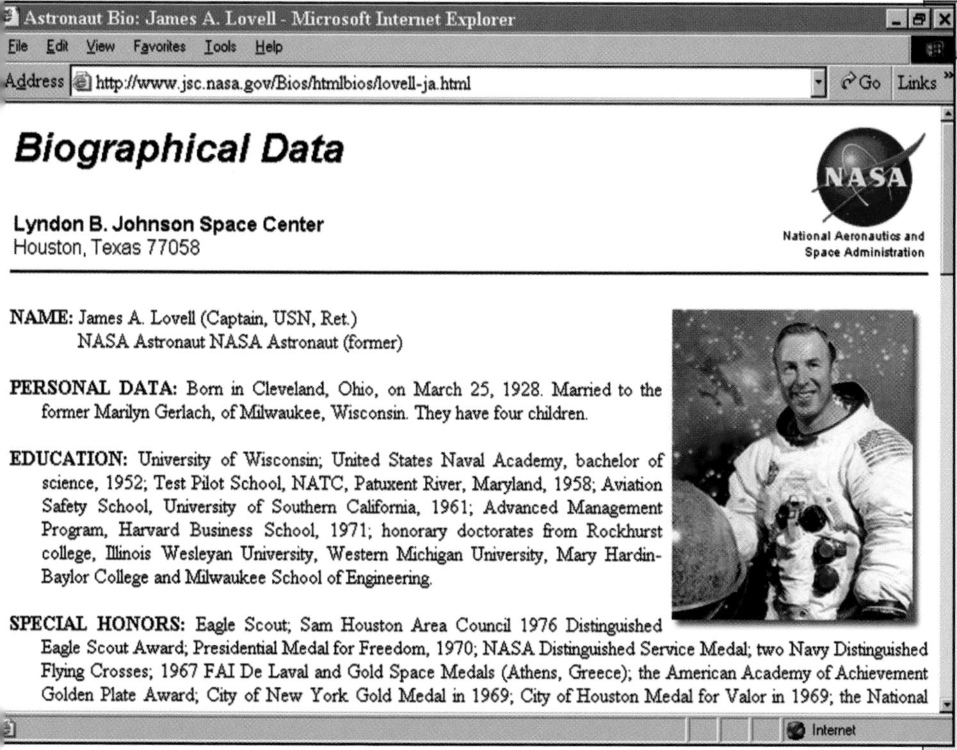

Astronaut Bio: James A. Lovell - Microsoft Internet Explorer

File   Edit   View   Favorites   Tools   Help

Address http://www.jsc.nasa.gov/Bios/htmlbios/lovell-ja.html   Go   Links

Biographical Data

Lyndon B. Johnson Space Center
Houston, Texas 77058

NASA
National Aeronautics and
Space Administration

NAME: James A. Lovell (Captain, USN, Ret.)
NASA Astronaut NASA Astronaut (former)

PERSONAL DATA: Born in Cleveland, Ohio, on March 25, 1928. Married to the former Marilyn Gerlach, of Milwaukee, Wisconsin. They have four children.

EDUCATION: University of Wisconsin; United States Naval Academy, bachelor of science, 1952; Test Pilot School, NATC, Patuxent River, Maryland, 1958; Aviation Safety School, University of Southern California, 1961; Advanced Management Program, Harvard Business School, 1971; honorary doctorates from Rockhurst college, Illinois Wesleyan University, Western Michigan University, Mary Hardin-Baylor College and Milwaukee School of Engineering.

SPECIAL HONORS: Eagle Scout; Sam Houston Area Council 1976 Distinguished Eagle Scout Award; Presidential Medal for Freedom, 1970; NASA Distinguished Service Medal; two Navy Distinguished Flying Crosses; 1967 FAI De Laval and Gold Space Medals (Athens, Greece); the American Academy of Achievement Golden Plate Award; City of New York Gold Medal in 1969; City of Houston Medal for Valor in 1969; the National

Internet

▲ *James A. Lovell (shown here) and Frank Borman served as the backup crew for the* Gemini 4 *space mission.*

in flight simulators filled many of their days. The mock flights tested the astronauts' responses to problems that could crop up during a mission. One moment, cabin pressure would drop. The next, the guidance system would break down. Gus Grissom later wrote, "All of us who flew the *Gemini* missions are pretty well agreed that the actual flights themselves seemed a lot easier than the simulations 'flown'. . . on the ground."[7]

The training did not stop there. High-speed dives in Air Force transports gave the astronauts brief tastes of weightlessness. The teams also simulated life in zero

gravity by working underwater in diving gear. Like the *Mercury* capsule, *Gemini* was designed to splash down at sea. If the spacecraft sank, the astronauts had to know how to escape. Once free of the ship, they had to prove they could handle a life raft. Planners also worried that a mishap could force the spacecraft to land far off track. One week the astronauts were set down in the desert, the next in a jungle. Each new "crash" site tested their survival skills.

▶ *Gemini 4* Gets a Crew

After long months of training, NASA chose the *Gemini* teams. No one would mistake the two Air Force majors picked to fly *Gemini 4* for twins, but the men were a good fit. Born within six months of each other, James A. "Jim" McDivitt and Edward H. "Ed" White II were the same height. Each man had a wife named Pat. After meeting at the University of Michigan in 1959, both trained as test pilots. McDivitt had flown combat missions in Korea, but White had logged more hours of flying time. In their spare time, both men enjoyed handball, golf, and swimming. As White put it, "Jim and I have been following right along together."[8]

In other ways, the two men were quite different. McDivitt was born in Chicago; White was born in San Antonio. The McDivitts had four children; the Whites had two. White came from a military family and was a West Point graduate. After serving in Korea, McDivitt had gone on to earn his college degree in aeronautics. As an astronaut, he played a key role in designing *Gemini's* guidance system. White took on the task of making sure the control system had a "pilot's touch." In 1962, each simulator was fitted with a different control stick. Think

▲ *James McDivitt was picked to be the command pilot of the Gemini 4 space mission. He would later serve as commander of Apollo 9.*

ahead to the moon missions, White cautioned. Why should astronauts be forced to use one kind of stick to get there, and a second to land the lunar module? The designers listened—and equipped all American spacecraft with the same control stick.[9]

When White was twelve, his pilot father allowed him to fly an old T–6 trainer. That first turn at the controls helped shape the boy's life. Years later, astronaut Ed White talked about the lesson he learned that day. "Set a goal," he said, "believe in your heart and soul that you can achieve it—and then work to accomplish it."[10]

Chapter 3

A LESSON IN ORBITAL PHYSICS

The long weeks of training ended at last. Early on the morning of June 3, 1965, Ed White and Jim McDivitt sat down to their preflight breakfast. While they ate steak and eggs, Cape Kennedy's launchpad LC–19 was buzzing with activity. Inside *Gemini*, the backup crew checked the ship's systems. Out on the pad, the ground crew pumped fuel into a giant Titan II rocket. By 7:07 A.M., the Titan was ready to go. When White and McDivitt climbed into the

▲ *Jim McDivitt (left) and Ed White (right) settle into their seats as they make final preparations for their flight in* Gemini 4.

spacecraft, their silvery space suits gleamed in the morning light.[1] Each suit displayed an American flag patch—a first for the space program.[2]

Around the world, television viewers hurried to turn on their sets. For the first time, a space launch was being broadcast live via Early Bird satellite, which allowed events filmed in North America to be viewed in Europe and around the globe. *Gemini 4*, the news reports promised, would score several "firsts." Space fans knew that this would be the first mission run from the new Mission Control Center in Houston. For the general public, Ed White's EVA was the big draw. NASA's approach to spaceflight was also on display. The Soviets used automated systems to fly their capsules. Cosmonauts never took over the controls unless a major system failed. By contrast, NASA trusted the skills of its former test pilots. *Gemini* astronauts were expected to take a hands-on role in flying their ships.[3]

Gemini Blasts Off

Only a single glitch marred the countdown. At thirty-five minutes before launch, the erector structure stuck while it was being lowered. Raised to its full height and lowered again, the erector jammed a second time. After a seventy-minute search, workers found and replaced a faulty connector. This time the erector lowered as planned. *Gemini 4* was ready.

The Titan II rocket ignited with a burst of orange flame at 10:16 A.M. Riding atop the powerful booster, *Gemini 4* blasted skyward. Inside the nearly silent cabin, McDivitt and White could feel their spacecraft gathering speed. Then, without warning, the rocket began to bounce like a pogo stick. In Houston, the flight controllers held their breath. If the bouncing continued, the rocket might break apart. Then, in the next instant, the "pogoing" stopped as quickly as it had begun. Everyone in Mission Control sighed with relief.[4]

Five-and-a-half minutes after liftoff, *Gemini 4* coasted into its planned orbit. At its apogee (highest point), the spacecraft was 175 miles (281 km) above the earth. The perigee (low point) checked out at 100 miles (162 km). By this time the booster's engines had cut off as planned. Twenty seconds later, McDivitt punched in the order to separate. As his ship pulled free, he used his thrusters to steer clear of the giant booster. A few minutes later, White spotted their fellow traveler about a hundred yards (91 m)

Astronaut Ed White emerges from the Gemini 4 capsule to take his historic spacewalk in this mock-up. This is on display at the National Air and Space Museum in Washington, D.C.

away. As called for in the flight plan, the astronauts set out to simulate a docking maneuver.[5]

▶ Losing Ground by Flying Faster

NASA's planners assumed that with the booster moving at a constant speed, *Gemini 4* could catch it by speeding up. Now, faced with a real space chase, all the old thinking went out the window. Their quarry, McDivitt and White reported, was tumbling along in a different orbit. If they moved in too close, they might crash into the booster. Despite the risk, the astronauts did their best to catch their target. Using thrusters to gain speed, they chased the booster toward their first dawn in space. Then, as the sun rose in a rainbow of colors, McDivitt called in a surprising report. The booster, he said, was farther away than ever.[6]

Moments later, the command pilot reported a new problem. "It's taken a little more fuel than we had anticipated," he told Mission Control. "Do you want me to really make a major effort to close . . . or to save the fuel?" The response came back almost at once. "I think we should save the fuel . . . I don't think it's worth it," Mission Director Chris Kraft said. McDivitt hated to give up the chase, but he knew the order made sense. "I'd like to save enough [fuel] to help bring me down," he told Kraft.[7]

In Houston, NASA engineers tackled the problem of the elusive booster. Speed and motion in orbit, they decided, do not follow earthly rules. In space, adding speed lifts the spacecraft into a higher orbit. When that happens, the faster moving ship falls farther and farther behind. Like a runner who takes the outside lane, *Gemini* lost ground because the higher the orbit, the longer it takes to circle the earth. The target vehicle, following a lower (and shorter) orbit, pulls farther and farther away. In later flights, *Gemini* pilots closed

 The Gemini 4 *spacecraft was blasted into orbit by a giant Titan II rocket.*

on their targets by dropping into lower, not higher, orbits. Only when they moved in close did they apply a burst of power. This final thrust allowed the chase ship to close in and dock with its target.[8]

Floating In Space

After failing to catch the booster, the astronauts turned to their next challenge—the EVA. As White assembled the gas gun, McDivitt went over the lengthy checklist. The first task done, White worked on the hookups for his tether and oxygen pack. As the minutes flew by, McDivitt noticed that his partner was looking tired. It would be safer, he thought, to postpone the spacewalk for another orbit. With Houston's okay, the astronauts took a break.

As *Gemini 4* soared over the Indian Ocean, White said he was ready. After struggling with the balky hatch cover, he set up his camera and floated into space. Like all astronauts, he was aware of the danger. If he blacked out, it was unlikely that McDivitt would be able to reel him back into the ship. In that case, the command pilot had orders to cut the spacewalker loose so he could seal the hatch. Buzz Aldrin, who would one day walk on the moon, explained the astronaut's feelings about risk. "We never believed we were doing anything extraordinarily dangerous," he said. "[We] were confident in our ability to do the job for which we were exceedingly well trained."[9]

After exhausting his gas gun, White used the tether to move around the spacecraft. "Changing my position by pulling on the tether was easy, like pulling a trout . . . out of a stream," he said later.[10] Inside the cabin, the tugs on the tether were keeping McDivitt busy. "When Ed gets out there and starts whipping around," the command

pilot told CapCom, "it sure makes the spacecraft tough to control."[11]

The suit was working well, and the helmet visor did a good job of shielding White's face from the sun's glare. "I can sit here and see the whole California coast," he told his worldwide audience. From inside the ship, McDivitt snapped photos of the spacewalker as he floated past. Clearly, White was having a great time. "I'm very thankful in having the experience to be first," the spacewalker said. "This is fun!"[12]

All too soon, the order came to end the spacewalk. White pulled himself back to the ship and climbed through the hatch. Closing the cover should have been a simple task, but the stubborn latch again refused to work. The long tether, coiling around the cabin like a snake, made the task even more difficult. When White pulled harder, the effort lifted him out of his seat. McDivitt reached over, grabbed his legs, and held on tight. As White fought with the cover, his pulse rate climbed to 178 beats a minute. Finally, the latch snapped shut. White dropped into his seat, tired and dripping with sweat—but supremely happy.

In Houston, the controllers took stock of the situation. The flight plan had called for the astronauts to reopen the hatch so they could toss out the EVA equipment. After the battle with the faulty latch, that seemed too risky. Capcom told White and McDivitt they would have to live with the tether and the rest of the gear for the next three days.

"PRIDE, PATRIOTISM, AND AMERICAN KNOW-HOW"

With *Gemini 4* buttoned up tight, McDivitt took a good look at his partner. White's faceplate, he saw, was fogged with sweat. The sight convinced him that they both needed a rest. In Houston, a big sigh of relief had echoed through Mission Control when the hatch snapped shut. Three teams were keeping a round-the-clock watch on the spacecraft. White Team leader Gene Kranz summed up the pride everyone was feeling. "This was one of those magical moments," he wrote. "Pride, patriotism, and American know-how triumphed that day. I was happy and proud, almost giddy, but then . . . it was time to get back to business."[1]

In the media center, reporters hurried to file their stories. A few spiced up their efforts by calling the ship *Little Eva*—a tribute to the nation's first EVA. Until this time, each capsule had been given its

Lieutenant Colonel Edward ▶
H. White II became the first American to carry out an EVA. His career was cut short in 1967 when a fire in Apollo 1*'s cabin took his life.*

own flight name. John Glenn made the first orbital flight in *Friendship 7*. *Gemini 3* had been christened the *Molly Brown*. McDivitt and White had wanted to call their ship *American Eagle,* but NASA refused. Naming the capsules, officials said, detracted from the serious nature of the missions.[2]

▷ Life in Orbit

After a short rest, the *Gemini 4* astronauts settled into a regular routine. Both men wore their G4C spacesuits throughout the mission. The suits protected the astronauts from radiation from the sun, as well as sudden changes in cabin temperature and pressure. With the cabin temperature holding at 75°F (24°C), McDivitt said he felt fine. White's suit, with its extra EVA layer, kept him a bit too warm. Six hours into the flight, both men complained of a strong odor that made their eyes burn. Mission Control guessed that the climate-control system was releasing the fumes. Later, the astronauts grumbled about their radio headsets. The lightweight headsets worked well enough— except when they floated off their heads at odd moments.[3]

On shorter flights, astronauts had shown some loss of muscle strength. Worried that the loss might be greater on a longer mission, doctors added a workout program for *Gemini 4*. The exerciser was a bungee cord with a handle at one end and a foot strap at the other. Nothing else would have worked in the tiny cabin. When the astronauts exercised, data flowed back to Houston from sensors embedded in their suits. The sensors kept track of pulse rates, blood pressure, and other vital signs. By the two-day mark, both men told CapCom they had lost interest in their workouts. They were more faithful in

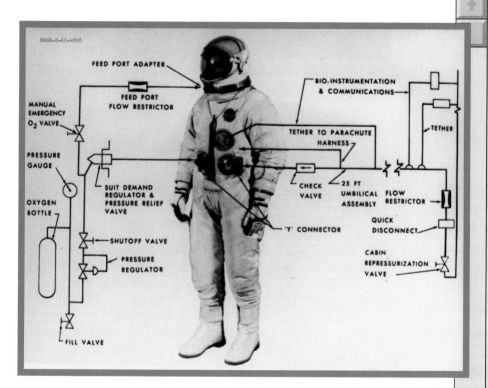

NASA-S-65-4865

FEED PORT ADAPTER

FEED PORT
FLOW RESTRICTOR

MANUAL
EMERGENCY
O₂ VALVE

PRESSURE
GAUGE

OXYGEN
BOTTLE

SUIT DEMAND
REGULATOR &
PRESSURE RELIEF
VALVE

SHUTOFF VALVE

PRESSURE
REGULATOR

FILL VALVE

BIO-INSTRUMENTATION
& COMMUNICATIONS

TETHER TO PARACHUTE
HARNESS

CHECK
VALVE

25 FT
UMBILICAL
ASSEMBLY

TETHER

FLOW
RESTRICTOR

QUICK
DISCONNECT

'Y' CONNECTOR

CABIN
REPRESSURIZATION
VALVE

▲ *A detailed view of the* Gemini *extravehicular space suit worn by Ed White.*

doing the stretching routines that relieved cramped leg and back muscles.[4]

For this first four-day flight, sleep and meal breaks had been added to the schedule. The plan was for one man to sleep while the other carried on his duties. When put to the test, however, the sleep schedule failed on all counts. Each time the on-duty astronaut moved, he disturbed the sleeper. To make matters worse, the cabin was anything but quiet. The radio crackled, thrusters fired with a whoosh, and power circuits hummed and buzzed. On later *Gemini* missions, the astronauts slept and ate at the same time.[5]

The flight plan also called for four meals a day. For the most part, "cooking" consisted of squirting water into packets of dried foods. To eat pot roast or chicken, the men squeezed the mushy mix into their mouths through a feed tube. The tastiest dish, they agreed, was smoked bacon. White, who loved big, juicy steaks, had to be content with this menu on the third day:

Breakfast—sugar-toasted flakes, sausage patties, cinnamon toast, orange-grapefruit juice.

Lunch—beef and gravy, cheese sandwich, apricot pudding, orange juice.

Dinner—beef pot roast, green peas, toasted bread cubes, pineapple cubes, tea.

Late dinner—Chicken bites, toast, applesauce, brownies, grapefruit juice.[6]

To prevent dehydration, doctors asked the men to drink at least two quarts (1.9 L) of fluids a day. At one point, the men's wives joined the doctors in urging their husbands to "drink up." Speaking from Mission Control, Pat White told Ed, "Have a drink of water."

"Roger," the dutiful husband replied. "Stand by for a drink of water."

Moments later, a second voice crackled through the headphones. "Hey, have a drink of water, both of you," Pat McDivitt ordered.[7]

The two Pats did not know that the men had not bothered to shave or brush their teeth. If they had known, they might have added a few commands about personal hygiene.

▲ This panorama of the Middle East, with the Suez Canal toward the center and Egypt sprawling across the lower half of the photo, was taken from Gemini 4. Ed White surprised NASA's experts when he reported that he could see city streets and factory smoke from space.

▶ Experiments and Observations

As the hours passed, the astronauts met another hazard of life in zero gravity. Each time a juice packet leaked, the droplets floated around the cabin. When they dug into a storage locker, the contents were sure to drift out. That meant catching each object (a gauge or a wrench, perhaps) and stowing it away again. If someone left a locker open, everything floated out all over again.

As the hours ticked by, McDivitt and White carried out a series of experiments. A dosimeter checked on radiation in the capsule. A magnetometer measured changes in the earth's magnetic fields. Another assignment called on their camera skills. As they passed over the United States, the astronauts snapped pictures of the landscape below. One set of photos gave weather experts a topside look at a big storm system. Turning their gaze skyward, the pilots used a sextant to check their position. A sextant measures the angular distance between two points in space, such as the sun and the horizon. The test confirmed that future crews could one day use sextants to help find their way to the moon and back.[8]

Around and above them, the *Gemini* twins glimpsed satellites and burned-out rockets. Looking down, they spotted Egypt's Nile River and the cities of Cairo and Alexandria. White said he could make out roads, streetlights, airfields, and smoke from factory chimneys. These sightings surprised the experts. Most had doubted that astronauts could see such small details from space.[9]

▶ "Like a Falling Rock"

As *Gemini 4* logged a record fourth day in space, CapCom ordered the crew to prepare for reentry. By now, McDivitt

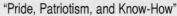

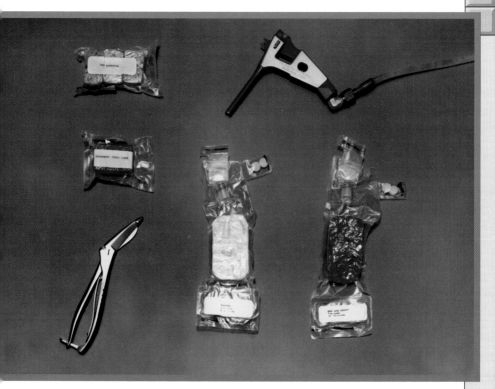

▲ *A dinner setting for the* Gemini 4 *astronauts. The photo shows packages of dried space food, a water gun to hydrate the food, and a pair of scissors to open the packages.*

had shown that he could maneuver *Gemini 4* with great precision. All seemed ready for him to fly the spacecraft to a gliding reentry. To do so, however, he needed the help of the ship's onboard computer. This was a first for an American spacecraft, and skeptics had warned that it might not work in space. The computer did work just fine—until day four. At that crucial moment, no matter how the men jiggled the switch, the computer did not respond. The failure left McDivitt with no choice but to make a plunging, *Mercury*-type reentry. To the command

pilot, that was like riding a falling rock back to Earth. "I just think it's old fashioned," he muttered.[10]

During orbit sixty-two, the astronauts fired *Gemini*'s retro-rockets. After plunging to an altitude of 16.8 miles (27 km), McDivitt slowed the roll rate and deployed the drogue parachute. A drogue parachute is designed to quickly slow things down as they fall. *Gemini 4* twisted and turned until the main chute popped open and further slowed the descent. Moments later, the ship splashed into the ocean. The impact slammed the two men around a bit, but they were down safely.

Due to the computer breakdown, the astronauts landed fifty miles (80 km) short of their target. Helicopters from the U.S.S. *Wasp*, however, reached them moments after splashdown. As *Gemini* bobbed in the waves, divers attached a flotation collar to keep it from sinking. McDivitt and White popped the hatch, jumped out, and climbed into a chopper. When they landed on the *Wasp*, the sailors rolled out a red carpet. The warm welcome, White said later, left him feeling "red, white, and blue all over."[11]

"A LONG STRIDE FORWARD"

Soon after White and McDivitt reached the *Wasp*, the captain called them to the phone. President Lyndon Johnson was on the other end of the line. "What you have done will never be forgotten," Johnson told them. "[You] two outstanding men have taken a long stride forward in mankind's progress."[1] To the American people, that "long stride forward" meant that the United States had jumped into the lead in the space race.

Before the astronauts left the *Wasp*, doctors ran them through a series of tests. The effects of weightlessness had been their biggest worry. A few had predicted that the pilots would faint—or even die—when they returned to Earth. To their surprise, neither astronaut showed signs of distress. Except for feeling tired and hungry, they were in good shape. White even danced a little jig when he stepped onto the red carpet. The tests did show that both men had lost some bone mass, but that was expected. Doctors also noted the fact that they had lost weight and their blood pressure had dropped.[2]

Four days in space left the astronauts badly in need of a shower. As White said with a smile, "I thought I smelled fine. It was all those people on the carrier that smelled strange."[3] While the tests dragged on, the astronauts found it hard to contain their high spirits. At one point, while lying on an X-ray table, McDivitt cut loose with a loud "Yahoo!"[4] On the second day, White joined in a tug-of-war

▲ *Ed White (left) and Jim McDivitt (right) returned home to high praise. President Lyndon B. Johnson phoned to congratulate them and promoted both astronauts to the rank of lieutenant colonel.*

between the ship's sailors and marines. His team lost, but his display of strength and endurance pleased the doctors.[5]

A Nearly Flawless Flight

With medical worries laid to rest, NASA drew up its balance sheet. *Gemini 4,* the record showed, met all but two of its objectives. Early in the flight, lack of fuel cut short the attempt to rendezvous with the booster. Four days later, the computer glitch kept McDivitt from flying the ship to a gliding reentry. As a joke, reporters gave the team an abacus (an ancient, handheld counting device). Use it, they said, if the computer conks out on future flights.[6]

For the most part, both men and machine performed flawlessly. At Mission Control, *Gemini 4*'s support teams proved they were ready to handle longer flights. While in orbit, the astronauts devoted twenty-two hours to eleven important experiments.[7] The high point, clearly, was White's spacewalk. His trouble-free EVA proved that astronauts could do useful work in space. The next big challenge, NASA's engineers agreed, would be the *Apollo* moon mission. After *Apollo*, their dream was to use spacewalkers to assemble an orbiting space platform.

Back in Houston, the astronauts families welcomed them with smiles and hugs. President Johnson pinned medals on both men and promoted them to lieutenant colonel. Then he sent them to represent the United States at the Paris Air Show. In France, Soviet cosmonaut Yuri Gagarin, revered as the first man to fly in space, shared the spotlight with the *Gemini* twins.[8] When White and McDivitt returned home, Chicago honored them with a tickertape parade. Not to be outdone, the University of Michigan gave them honorary doctorate degrees. Their

http://grin.hq.nasa.gov/IMAGES/SMALL/GPN-2002-000151.jpg - Microsoft Internet Explorer

File   Edit   View   Favorites   Tools   Help

Address http://grin.hq.nasa.gov/IMAGES/SMALL/GPN-2002-000151.jpg   Go   Links

Done   Internet

▲ Soviet cosmonaut Yuri Gagarin (left) shakes hands with the crew of *Gemini 4. Gagarin was the first human to fly in space as well as the first human to orbit Earth.*

new degrees entitled the astronauts to be called Dr. White and Dr. McDivitt.

▷ Opening Doors to the Future

Gemini 4 set a bundle of new space records, from total flight time to time spent in EVA. Then, one by one, those records tumbled. Each new *Gemini* mission pushed ahead, building on what earlier flights had achieved. By the time *Gemini 12* splashed down in November 1966, the United States was well out in front in the space race. President Johnson spoke of the successes when he said, "Ten times in . . . the last twenty months we have placed two men in orbit . . . ten times we have brought them home."[9] Thanks to *Gemini*, NASA was ready to push ahead with the *Apollo* moon lander program.

Ed White and Jim McDivitt saw *Apollo* as their ticket for more trips into space. For White, that assignment ended in tragedy. On January 27, 1967, he joined Gus Grissom and Roger Chaffee in the command module of *Apollo 1*. During the countdown, an electric spark started an intensely hot fire in the cabin. A few seconds later, all three astronauts were dead. NASA went back to the drawing board to rethink its safety rules.[10]

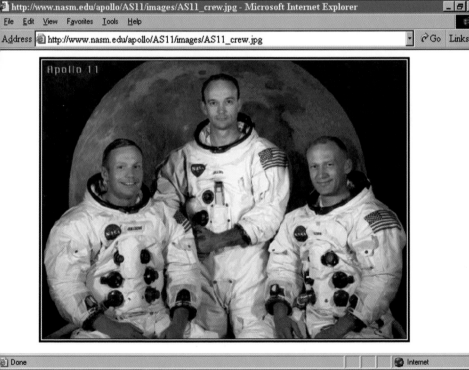

▲ *The crew of* Apollo 11 *could not have accomplished the first lunar landing without the knowledge gained by* Gemini 4 *and other space missions. From left to right are* Apollo 11 *astronauts Neil Armstrong, Michael Collins, and Buzz Aldrin.*

▲ Astronaut Ed White floats peacefully over the distant Earth. Far below, New Mexico spins past him in this photo snapped by Command Pilot Jim McDivitt.

McDivitt returned to space on March 3, 1969, as *Apollo 9*'s command pilot. During their ten days in Earth orbit, McDivitt, Rusty Schweickart, and Dave Scott gave the lunar module a tough workout. The big test came on their fifth day in space. McDivitt and Schweickart backed the fragile-looking module clear of the *Apollo 9* command ship and flew off into the inky blackness. After simulating an ascent from the moon's surface, they returned to Scott in the command ship. As the docking mechanism snapped into place, cheers erupted in Houston's control center. All the pieces were in place. It was only a matter of time before a team of astronauts landed on the moon.[11] Six months later, *Apollo 11* carried Neil Armstrong, Buzz Aldrin, and Michael Collins on their historic mission. On July 20, Armstrong and Aldrin flew the lunar lander to a soft landing on the moon.

"Houston, Tranquility Base here. The Eagle has landed," Armstrong told a waiting world.[12] Without a doubt, it was *Apollo*'s show. Back on Earth, however, the *Gemini* crews must have felt that they, too, were part of that great moment.

Chapter 1. An American Spacewalk

1. Peter Bond, *Heroes in Space; from Gagarin to Challenger* (New York: Basil Blackwell, Inc., 1987), p. 90.

2. Ibid.

3. Anthony J. Cipriano, *America's Journeys into Space; the Astronauts of the United States* (New York: Julian Messner, 1979), p. 32.

4. Bond, p. 91.

5. David J. Shayler, *Gemini; Steps to the Moon* (Chichester, UK: Praxis Publishing, 2001), p. 277.

6. Ibid., p. 278.

7. Gene Kranz, *Failure Is Not an Option; Mission Control from Mercury to Apollo 13 and Beyond* (New York: Simon & Schuster, 2000), p. 140.

Chapter 2. Embarking on a Great Adventure

1. Patrick J. Walsh, *Echoes Among the Stars; a Short History of the U.S. Space Program* (Armonk, N.Y: M. E. Sharpe, 2000), p. 22.

2. Ibid., p. 13.

3. Peter Bond, *Heroes in Space; from Gagarin to Challenger* (New York: Basil Blackwell, Inc., 1987), p. 83.

4. United Press International, *Gemini; America's Historic Walk in Space* (Englewood Cliffs, N.J.: Prentice-Hall, Inc., 1965), chapter 1.

5. "Gemini 4; 1st American Space Walk," *Mission History; Detailed Account of the Gemini IV Mission,* May 10, 2000, <http://www/thespaceplace.com/history/Gemini/gemini04.html> (December 5, 2002).

6. Virgil "Gus" Grissom, *Gemini; a Personal Account of Man's Venture into Space* (New York: The Macmillan Company, 1968), pp. 86–87.

7. Ibid., p. 84.

8. Mary C. Zornio, "Detailed Biographies of Apollo I Crew— Ed White," *NASA History,* February 3, 2003, <http://www.nasa.gov/office/pao/History/Apollo204/zorn/white.htm> (April 11, 2003).

9. Ibid.

10. Ibid.

Chapter 3. A Lesson in Orbital Physics

1. Barton C. Hacker and James M. Grimwood, "Four Days and a 'Walk'," *On the Shoulders of Titans: A History of Project Gemini,* n.d., <http://www.hq.nasa.gov/office/pao/History/Sp-4203/ch11-2.htm>, (April 11, 2003).

2. Timothy B. Benford and Brian Wilkes, *The Space Program Quiz & Fact Book* (New York: Harper & Row, Publishers, 1985), p. 53.

3. Patrick J. Walsh, *Echoes Among the Stars; a Short History of the U.S. Space Program* (Armonk, N.Y.: M. E. Sharpe, 2000), p. 15.

4. Gene Kranz, *Failure Is Not an Option; Mission Control from Mercury to Apollo 13 and Beyond* (New York: Simon & Schuster, 2000), p. 137.

5. Ibid.

6. United Press International, *Gemini; America's Historic Walk in Space* (Englewood Cliffs, N.J.: Prentice-Hall, Inc., 1965), chapter 2.

7. Ibid.

8. Hacker and Grimwood.

9. Dr. Fred Kelly, *America's Astronauts and Their Indestructible Spirit* (Blue Ridge Summit, Pa.: Tab Books, Inc., 1986), p. vii.

10. Peter Bond, *Heroes in Space; from Gagarin to Challenger* (New York: Basil Blackwell, Inc., 1987), p. 83.

11. William Shelton, *American Space Exploration: The First Decade* (Boston: Little, Brown and Co., 1967), p. 279.

12. Mary C. Zornio, "Detailed Biographies of Apollo I Crew— Ed White," *NASA History,* February 3, 2003, <http://www.nasa.gov/office/pao/History/Apollo204/zorn/white.htm> (April 11, 2003).

13. Virgil "Gus" Grissom, *Gemini: A Personal Account of Man's Venture Into Space* (Englewood Cliffs, N.J.: Prentice-Hall, Inc., 1965), p. 222.

Chapter 4. "Pride, Patriotism, and American Know-How"

1. Gene Kranz, *Failure Is Not an Option; Mission Control from Mercury to Apollo 13 and Beyond* (New York: Simon & Schuster, 2000), p. 139.

2. Barton C. Hacker and James M. Grimwood, "Four Days and a 'Walk'," *On the Shoulders of Titans: A History of Project Gemini,* n.d., <http://www.hq.nasa.gov/office/pao/History/Sp-4203/ch11-2.htm> (April 11, 2003).

3. David J. Shayler, *Gemini; Steps to the Moon* (Chichester, UK: Praxis Publishing, 2001), p. 205.

4. Ibid.

5. Peter Bond, *Heroes in Space; from Gagarin to Challenger* (New York: Basil Blackwell, Inc., 1987), p. 93.

6. United Press International, *Gemini; America's Historic Walk in Space* (Englewood Cliffs, N.J.: Prentice-Hall, Inc., 1965), chapter 4.

7. Ibid.

8. Mark Wade, *Gemini 4,* June 26, 2002, <http://www.astronautix.com/flights/gemini4.htm> (April 11, 2002).

9. Bond, p. 93.

10. United Press International, chapter 4.

11. Timothy B. Benford and Brian Wilkes, *The Space Program Quiz & Fact Book* (New York: Harper & Row, 1985), p. 23.

Chapter 5. "A Long Stride Forward"

1. United Press International, *Gemini; America's Historic Walk in Space* (Englewood Cliffs, N.J.: Prentice-Hall, Inc., 1965), chapter 4.

2. Peter Bond, *Heroes in Space; from Gagarin to Challenger* (New York: Basil Blackwell, Inc., 1987), p. 94.

3. Mary C. Zornio, "Detailed Biographies of Apollo I Crew— Ed White," *NASA History*, February 3, 2003, <http://www.nasa.gov/office/pao/History/Apollo204/zorn/white.htm> (April 11, 2003).

4. United Press International, chapter 4.

5. David J. Shayler, *Gemini; Steps to the Moon* (Chichester, UK: Praxis Publishing, 2001), p. 206.

6. Bond, p. 94.

7. Shayler, p. 338.

8. Zornio.

9. Shayler, p. 399.

10. Bond, p. 139.

11. Chris Kraft, *Flight: My Life in Mission Control* (New York: Dutton, 2001), pp. 305–306.

12. James Schefter, *The Race; the Complete True Story of How America Beat Russia to the Moon* (New York: Anchor Books, 2000), p. 286.

Further Reading

Kallen, Stuart A. *Gemini Spacewalkers.* Edina, Minn.: ABDO Publishing Company, 1996.

Kranz, Gene. *Failure Is Not an Option; Mission Control from Mercury to Apollo 13 and Beyond.* New York: Simon & Schuster, 2000.

Schefter, James. *The Race; the Complete True Story of How America Beat Russia to the Moon.* New York: Anchor Books, 2000.

Shayler, David J. *Gemini: Steps to the Moon.* Chichester, UK: Praxis Publishing, 2001.

Spangenburg, Ray and Kit Moser. *Project Gemini.* Danbury, Conn.: Franklin Watts, 2001.

Stott, Carole. *Space Exploration.* New York: Dorling Kindersley Publishing, 1997.

Vogt, Gregory L. *Spacewalks: The Ultimate Adventure in Orbit.* Berkeley Heights, N.J.: Enslow Publishers, Inc., 2000.

Walsh, Patrick J. *Echoes Among the Stars: A Short History of the U.S. Space Program.* Armonk, N.Y.: M. E. Sharpe, 2000.

Zelon, Helen. *The First American Space Walk: The Gemini IV Mission.* New York: PowerKids Press, 2002.

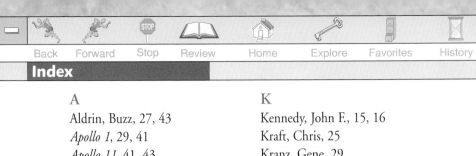

Index